SPERM WHALES

by Victor Gentle and Janet Perry

Gareth Stevens Publishing
A WORLD ALMANAC EDUCATION GROUP COMPANY

04 2/03

Please visit our web site at: www.garethstevens.com
For a free color catalog describing Gareth Stevens' list of high-quality books and
multimedia programs, call 1-800-542-2595 (USA) or 1-800-461-9120 (Canada).
Gareth Stevens Publishing's Fax: (414) 332-3567.

Library of Congress Cataloging-in-Publication Data

Gentle, Victor.
    Sperm whales / by Victor Gentle and Janet Perry.
       p. cm. — (Whales and dolphins: an imagination library series)
    Includes bibliographical references and index.
    ISBN 0-8368-2885-2 (lib. bdg.)
    1. Sperm whale—Juvenile literature. [1. Sperm whale. 2. Whales.]
I. Perry, Janet, 1960- II. Title.
QL737.C435G46   2001
599.5'47—dc21   2001025014

First published in 2001 by
Gareth Stevens Publishing
A World Almanac Education Group Company
330 West Olive Street, Suite 100
Milwaukee, WI 53212 USA

Text: Victor Gentle and Janet Perry
Art direction: Karen Knutson
Page layout: Victor Gentle, Janet Perry, Joel Bucaro, and Tammy Gruenewald
Cover design: Joel Bucaro
Series editor: Catherine Gardner
Picture Researcher: Diane Laska-Swanke

Photo credits: Cover, pp. 7 (insets), 15, 17 © Doug Perrine/Seapics.com; p. 5 © O. Louis
Mazzatenta/NGS Image Collection; p. 7 (main) © Seapics.com; p. 9 © IFAW/Seapics.com;
p. 11 © Else Bostelman/NGS Image Collection; p. 13 © Mark Carwardine/Seapics.com;
p. 19 © Flip Nicklin/Minden Pictures; p. 21 © Robert Pitman/Seapics.com; p. 22 Joel
Bucaro/© Gareth Stevens, Inc., 2001

Printed in the United States of America

1 2 3 4 5 6 7 8 9 05 04 03 02 01

Front cover: This sperm whale swims in the cold waters of the
North Atlantic. Male sperm whales grow to more than 50 feet
(15.2 meters) long. Females grow to more than 35 feet (10.7 m).

TABLE OF CONTENTS

Words that appear in the glossary are printed in **boldface** type the first time they occur in the text.

HOW CLOSE TO EXTINCTION?

At one time, millions of sperm whales lived in our oceans. In the 1800s, people began to hunt these magnificent creatures in a big way. By 1900, whalers had killed three-fourths of the world's sperm whales.

Early whalers hunted mostly females and **calves**, which were easier to find and catch than male sperm whales. With bigger and faster ships, modern whalers could catch and kill the bigger males. Scientists worry there may be too few males left for the **species** to survive.

Sperm whales breed slowly, producing only one **calf** every five years. Females must be 9 years old and males must reach 20 before they can mate. Does all this math mean that the sperm whale's days on the planet are numbered?

A whaler is ready to harpoon a sperm whale. Some nations still hunt them. How can sperm whales possibly recover while they are still under attack?

SOUND HEADS

Sperm whales are famous for their very big heads, which are about a third of their body length. They have the biggest brains on the planet. But sperm whales were not hunted for their brains — or even for their meat. They were hunted mainly for the fine oil from their **spermaceti** organ.

The spermaceti organ is a long sac in a sperm whale's head. It is filled with spermaceti, a liquid wax that is also called "sperm oil." Beneath it is a group of sacs filled with fat. These sacs are called the "**junk**," because whalers had no use for them.

The spermaceti organ and the junk seem to be key parts of the sperm whale's sound system. Sound is a sperm whale's most important tool.

Nineteenth-century whalers strip the flesh off a sperm whale. The small pictures show old candles made from sperm oil and an antique bottle of sperm oil.

"SEEING" WITH SOUND

If you swim with sperm whales, you will hear three different noises: **clicks**, **creaks**, and **clangs**. They use each noise in a different way.

Underwater, sperm whales make loud clicks and then listen for the echoes. This is called **echolocation**, and they use it almost all the time. It is their way of "looking around," using sound instead of sight. Eyesight is not nearly as good as sound for finding stuff in deep, dark water.

After a sperm whale "spots" an object with its clicks, it zeroes in on the object with creaks. Creaks are a rapid series of clicks. Echoes from the creaks show the object and its motion in fine detail. If the object is a squid, yummy! If it is a rock, yawn!

A researcher approaches a group of sperm whales. Close up, they would be able to see her. At a distance, they would be able to hear their clicks echo off her body.

GIANT SQUID FOR SUPPER?

Some whales have teeth, and some do not. Instead of teeth, **baleen** whales have large, stiff plates that act like strainers. They also have small throats, so they must eat tiny sea creatures — millions of them.

Toothed whales eat much bigger **prey** than baleen whales eat. Sperm whales are the largest toothed whales. Using echolocation, they hunt squid, sharks, and other deep-sea creatures, big and small. Sperm whales need to eat about a ton of food a day. You would, too, if you had such a big body to feed.

The most fearsome food that a sperm whale eats is the giant squid — a monster with razor-edged suckers and a huge beak. A sperm whale's skin often has scars from fierce battles with giant squid.

Sperm whales have circle-shaped battle scars from fights with giant squid. Usually they wrestle in the inky depths of the ocean, not on the surface as this painting shows.

MASTERS OF THE DEEP

Sperm whales dive deeper and hold their breath longer than any other air-breathing animal, including other whales. They can hold their breath well over an hour. Humans can hold their breath for just a few minutes.

Sperm whales can dive to 8,200 feet (2,500 m). At this depth, the pressure is about 250 times as powerful as on the surface. This pressure can crush all but the sturdiest scientific submarines. The record dive for a human without any special equipment is a very dangerous 417 feet (127 m).

Why do sperm whales make such extraordinary dives? They must — that is where their food lives!

Tail raised, this sperm whale begins a deep-sea dive in the South Pacific near New Zealand. It may be gone for up to an hour feeding near the ocean floor.

CHAT OR CHALLENGE?

Clicking helps sperm whales keep track of each other, as well as check out their surroundings. One may "overhear" when another has found a scrumptious squid or another good source of food.

Sperm whales click to **communicate**, too. When they hang out, they use rhythmic patterns of clicks, called **codas**. They seem to be talking with each other. Sperm whales from different parts of the world use different codas.

Clangs are very loud clicks that send a different kind of message, but whale experts are not sure what that message is. A male sperm whale clangs as he swims up to a group of females. He might be trying to impress the ladies or warn off other males.

These sperm whales are socializing — playing together, touching, and communicating. Family groups get together for two to three hours every day.

GROWING UP

Females and calves live together in groups. Twenty whales in a group is not unusual. When a mother goes on a long dive, her calf is protected by adults at the surface. If they did not "baby-sit" like this, the calf might be easy prey for killer whales or a large shark.

Males leave the mixed group when they are about six years old. They form smaller groups of their own, with 2 to 10 males. For the next 10 to 15 years, they stay in the colder feeding grounds. When the males have grown big enough to attract females, they move to the warmer breeding grounds.

Many large males have scars from other males. These scars may have come from fights for the right to visit groups of females in the breeding grounds.

A sperm whale calf, like this one, is protected by "baby-sitters" while its mother is away on a deep dive. In case of danger, any nearby adult will protect it.

GIRLS AND BOYS

The differences between adult females and adult males are greater for sperm whales than for any other whales. Females are about two-thirds as long as males and weigh about one-third as much. Females weigh about 30,000 pounds (13,600 kilograms). Males weigh about 95,000 pounds (43,100 kg).

When a male clangs and approaches a group of females, they are not put off by his size. They crowd around, roll their bodies along his, and make quite a fuss. They are happy to see him — especially these days. Male sperm whales are quite rare.

The slaughter of males in the twentieth century threatens the survival of the species. But hunting is not the only serious threat that these whales face.

Two females and two calves greet a male on a rare visit. He may have scars from his fights with other males, but in female company, he is the perfect gentleman.

SPERM WHALES IN DANGER

Today, there may be about 500,000 sperm whales left. That may seem like plenty of sperm whales. It is not. They reproduce slowly. The number of sperm whales can grow only by one percent in a year — *if all threats to them are removed.*

There are many dangers. Collisions with ships kill many sperm whales. **Pollution** poisons the food they eat. This can kill them outright or weaken their ability to fight disease. Noise pollution may make it hard for them to use their echolocation, which they need to find food and mates.

With all these dangers, the number of sperm whales might still drop, even if we stopped hunting them. Protecting them from whalers is just the first step.

Sickness from pollution may cause sperm whales to swim toward the shore and become stranded, as they did on this beach in Oregon in 1979.

MORE TO READ AND VIEW

Books (Nonfiction)   *Library of the Oceans.* (Grolier)
Little Irvy, the Tale of a Whale.
   Tyrone Malone, as told to Margaret Church (Children's Press)
Warrior Whale. Joseph J. Cook (Dodd Mead)
Whales and Dolphins (series). Victor Gentle and Janet Perry
   (Gareth Stevens)
Whales and Other Marine Mammals. George S. Fichter (Golden Books)

Books (Fiction)   *Amigo, the Friendly Gray Whale.* A. Kay Lay (Waterborne Press)
   [includes songs and a CD]
Baby Whale's Journey. Jonathan London (Chronicle)
Little Calf. Victor Sheffer (Scribner)
Thor, the Last of the Sperm Whales. Robert McClung (Morrow)
The Wild Whale Watch. Eva Moore (Scholastic)

Videos (Nonfiction)   *The Great Whales.* (National Geographic)
Spouts Ahoy! (BBC)

SPERM WHALE QUICK FACTS

Average weight of adults
Females: 30,000 pounds (13,600 kg)
Males: 95,000 pounds (43,100 kg)

Average length of adults
Females: 36 feet (11.0 m)
Males: 52 feet (15.8 m)

Number of teeth
Lower: 36 to 50 teeth, from 3 to 8 inches
  (7.6 to 20.3 centimeters) long; no upper teeth visible

Length of life
About 70 years

Special features
They can dive to 8,200 feet (2,500 m) and hold their breath more
than an hour. Their head is about one-third of their body length.

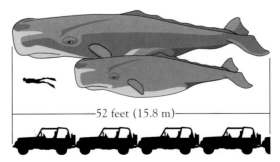

—52 feet (15.8 m)—

WEB SITES

If you have your own computer and Internet access, great! If not, most libraries have Internet access. The Internet changes every day, and web sites come and go. We believe the following sites are likely to last and give the best, most appropriate links for readers to find out more about the oceans, whales, and other sea life.

To get started, enter the word "museums" in a general search engine. See if you can find a museum web page that has exhibits on ocean mammals and oceanography. If any of these museums are close to home, you can visit them in person!

www.yahooligans.com
This is a huge search engine and a great research tool for anything you might want to know. For information on whales, click on Animals under the Science & Nature heading. From the Animals page, you can hear or see whales and dolphins by clicking on Animal Sounds or Animal Pictures.

Or you may want to plug some words into the search engine to see what Yahooligans can find for you. Some words related to sperm whales are echolocation and giant squid.

www.discovery.com/guides/animals/ under_water.html
Browse through information about many underwater creatures. Don't miss the topics Quest for the Giant Squid, Whale Attack, and

Long-Distance Calls: Voices of the Great Whales. You'll read the latest information, see up-close photographs, and take amazing underwater tours.

www.enchantedlearning.com/
Go to Zoom School and click on Whale Activities and Whale Dictionary for games, information sheets, and great links for many species of whales.

www.whaleclub.com
The *Whale Club* is a great place to go to talk to other whale fans, talk to whale experts, and find out the latest news about whales.

whale.wheelock.edu
The *WhaleNet* is packed full of the latest whale research information. Some is way cool! Click on the Students and then the WhaleNet Index button to find more buttons and links that will help you find whale videos, hear echolocation, or ask a whale expert a question.

www.mbayaq.org/lc/kids_place/kidseq.asp
Make postcards, play games, find out about marine science careers, and more!

GLOSSARY

You can find these words on the pages listed. Reading a word in a sentence helps you understand it even better.

baleen (buh-LEEN) — plates of fingernail-like material that hang in the mouths of some whales and strain food from sea water 10

calf (KAF) — a baby whale; plural: **calves** (KAVZ) 4, 16

clang (KLAYNG) — a loud sound that male sperm whales make when they approach a group of females 8, 14, 18

click (KLIK) — a sound made by sperm whales, used in echolocation and talking with their fellow whales 8, 14

codas (KOH-duhs) — patterns of clicks that sperm whales use to talk with other sperm whales 14

communicate (kuh-MYOO-nuh-kayt) — to share information or comfort 14

creak (KREEK) — a fast series of clicks used by sperm whales in echolocation 8

echolocation (EK-oh-loh-KAY-shun) — the process of sending and receiving sound to learn about an object or an animal 8, 10, 20

junk (JUNGK) — group of fatty, lens-shaped organs located in a sperm whale's head 6

pollution (puh-LOO-shun) — poisons put into or onto the land, air, or water 20

prey (PRAY) — animals that are hunted for food 10, 16

species (SPEE-shees) — a group of plants or animals that are like each other in many ways 4, 18

spermaceti (spurm-a-SEE-tee) — the liquid wax found in a long sac located in a sperm whale's head 6

INDEX

24